AWAKE WITH CONSCIOUS THOUGHTS

Lincoln Robinson

Awake with Conscious Thoughts

Copyright © 2022 by Lincoln Robinson

All rights reserved. No part of this book may be reproduced or transmitted in any form or by any means without written permission of the author.

ISBN 978-0-9845572-9-5

CONTENTS

Dedication..1

The Creation 5
Postive Healing...7
Shine Like a Star...9
New Dimension 11
Positivity 13
Believe 15
Soaring Confession 17
Generously Giving 19
Human You One No Way 21
Shining Bright 23
You Will..25
The Spirit "Now"...27
Another Sunny Day 29
That's a Plus..31
After All These Years 33
Power Facts 35
Proud Parents...37
Shifted Universe...39
It's a New Day 41
Cease and Settle 43

DEDICATION

GIFT #2

In loving memory of my first-born son, Daniel. There's a beacon of light that always shines bright, so I am granted guidance along the way, you always shine like a star cause that's who you are. Your light is never done.

Daniel

From the very first day that your amazing, powerful, bright light, lit up my heart; that light never seems to dimmer. I always feel your amazing, intelligent, caring warm hearted spirit, in and around me. You remain a part of my soul. Thanks for being such a delightful inspiration to everyone. I am always thinking of you, my son.

> In Loving Memory,
> Your Dad

GIFT # 1

To my daughter

Nakesha, you're an angel that brings forth joy. Having a daughter as beautiful as you are, is a wonderful experience. Just the very thought of your existence, your strong-minded personality, your great choice in a loving husband, Kevin, makes life more exciting and rewarding with each new day. You both have blessed me with two of the most extraordinary granddaughters, Ajale and Janai; two beautiful souls. Your continuous accomplishments give joy to my existence, truly fulfilling my conscious thoughts. Your special spirit is a gift to me on this amazing journey. I am so proud of you, and I am forever loving you with all my heart.

Love,
Your Dad

GIFT # 3 & 4

To my two distinguished Sons
Devon and Dorian

My two golden cornerstones; you are both the building blocks that keep my structure firmly planted. Your mannerly and humble spirits defy expectations. So ambitious, so distinguished, so courageous and intelligent. The gratification I receive each day as I rise, I can lift my head up high and breathe in the positive energy you both release into the universe. The creator has truly created two of the most incredible beings who physically and mentally continue to display such kingly character. I've always envisioned a bright future for you both. It is an honor to have been given the gift of representing you both as your father.

    Strongly loving you both always,
    Your Dad

THE CREATION

The CREATOR of creation has created the most ultimate creation.
Ignited fire from a spark, powerful light was created in this endless universe,
with the everlasting vibration of bright energy, enough for all of creation.

Created was the sun that lights the sky,
the moon, whose reflection of the sun, gives us its light by night.
Also, wind that pushes water-filled clouds, which bring forth showers of life-giving sustenance
falling upon the earth, blessing her with all that is needed in creation.
Amazingly, all that is created is a vessel,
that's fully energized with supernatural instinct to survive in creation.

Limitless amounts of consciousness, wisdom, and knowledge is given to all that is created.
It's so wonderful to know that the only obligation that's ordained by the CREATOR
is that all of creation exist in harmony and show love to all that is created.

POSTIVE HEALING

May the blessing of healing be restored upon us
through thought, belief, and the high vibration
of positive energy, that's granted unto us in abundance
by the MOST HIGH and mighty, the CREATOR.

SHINE LIKE A STAR

In these times of uncertainty one thing is for sure,
lots of minds are crated, locked up and gated,
can't seem to find their way out.
Living like sheeples, and not real people,
not even willing to open their mouth.
Can't always whisper and display doubt,
sometimes we have to shout.
Wake up in the morning, it's bright and shining,
that light is called the sun.
Can follow its lead and plan to succeed, the day has
    just begun.
Open your eyes and you will see, there's still lots of ways
    to get things done.
Must know your true purpose, stay strong and focus,
no reason to build up doubt, it's not hard to figure
    things out.
Must lose the frustration that negative notion, life is not
    over till it's done.
Put your feet down and turn things around,
you can walk, you don't have to run.
You must stand tall and give it you all, be wise and
    follow the sun.
Must shine like a star, cause that's who you are.
Your light is never done.

NEW DIMENSION

While moving in this new dimension,
a few things needing to be mentioned,
must be in control of your own destination,
a direct purpose and conscious meditation.

Avoiding all negative distraction and illusion,
not to mention those overwhelming, useless thoughts of confusion.

After such a long time of enforced indoctrination, not just on me, entire nations.
So fortunate to be one of the first chosen to gracefully enter this new dimension.

Spiritually energized with wisdom and determination,
knowing thyself, full of confidence and inspiration,
realizing the endless amount of provision prepared for me, there is no limitation.

Endless sunshine and positive vibration shining down brightly on me,
as I travel through this new dimension.

POSITIVITY

Smoking my chalice and sipping on wine,
thinking that everything is gonna be fine.
Then I go inside my mind to find
a great big world that has been swept behind.
I think of all the things to do
and some bad light comes and paints my thoughts blue.
Negativity versus positivity, there's got to be change to
    make it through.

YOU GOT TO BE POSITIVE!

Like a pyramid, strong from the bottom straight
    to the top,
there is no way they can make me drop.

YOU GOT TO BE POSITIVE!

Sometimes I wonder, my mind ponders
how they spread such propaganda.
And now the truth comes to light;
things that were cloudy now shine bright.

YOU GOT TO BE POSITIVE!

They try to hypnotize my mind only to find that I am
    so strong.
I am one of a kind, strong from the bottom straight
    to the top
like a pyramid I'll never drop.

YOU GOT TO BE POSITIVE!

BELIEVE

Believe in yourself.

In the power you must control your own spirit.

Day by day, believe in the strength you have deep inside.

Believe in tomorrow, and what it will bring.

Let a generous heart carry you through.

Things will work out if you trust your heart and believe.

There's no limit to what you can do.

SOARING CONFESSION

Thinking highly of only me while soaring high and free,
way too fast and too far up to see.

Spreading my wings, as I did my thing, soaring from
    high above,
feeling cold while losing my soul, like a featherless dove.
Didn't take heed while breaking hearts, showing far too
    little love.

Heart was hollow and empty, feeling lust, thirsty.
My mind just couldn't stay up,
and like a volcano filled with pressure, I blow my top
    and erupt.
From the fallout dust in my eyes, blinded couldn't see,
all so foggy, hope was lost, nothing left for me.

As I gather my thoughts, I suddenly rise and open my
    eyes to see
to my surprise, another miracle; my defender waiting
    just for me.
That special spirit of HIMSELF was granted unto me.

Once again, with a clean heart and a fresh start, has
    freed me like a dove.
From now on, I'm soaring with love, correcting all the
    things above.

GENEROUSLY GIVING

Meaningful things pass us by on the fly as other soul's cry,
and while most are flying high, others are let down and left to die.
It's a good thing that spirits are set free and for that I am so sure,
the great ones are always with me, day by day I can feel them more and more.

I can feel that peaceful energy that inspires my soul,
even at night after I have closed my door to feel secure.
Having the knowledge that I was created from that special mold,
gives me the courage to face another day as it unfolds.

Knowing that a good gesture and a smile can lift up another soul,
each day on my journey I make that my special goal.
Generously giving to all those who need me
so grateful I am blessed, not having to beg any one to feed me,
I give all I can to the poor and the needy.

So, to all the great spirits that continue to guide me,
I give thanks for the appreciation that is returned to me so abundantly speedy.

HUMAN YOU ONE NO WAY

You would think that the word "human" might have meant you one, but no way.
Unlike other species of the earth, we claim to be more intelligent.
So intelligent that we always try to outsmart each other, and always end up outsmarting ourselves.
And if we are challenged, no one wants to be the loser.
How selfish we live our lives from day to day when things are going our way.
And only when things and times get bad, so fast we turn to pray.
Human You One No way.

SHINING BRIGHT

In this higher state of consciousness, it's amazing
    to be thee,
since knowledge is the greatest key that I will
    bring with me,
with this mighty hand of wisdom, I will set my
    spirit free.

Everything is possible; the light is shining bright for me.
Don't see many obstacles. No need to fall on
    bended knees.
Up ahead is love and happiness as far as I can see.

From now on, moving forward with conscious
    grace and love.
Giving thanks to the CREATOR for the moon and
    stars above.

Thanks for the energy that's granted me.
Lots of peace and love.

YOU WILL

You will have a brighter day when you smile and show love along the way.

You should answer when you're called and be thankful for it all.

You will always do quite well if you never cast a bad spell.

You will always pass the test when you do better than the rest.

You can show how much you care when you treat all others fair.

You will only trip and stumble when you're not very humble.

You'll never get things done if you are always on the run.

You can always stop and rest after you've done your very best.

After all is said and done, go celebrate and have some fun.

THE SPIRIT "NOW"

The Spirit does not compromise.
The Spirit will only jeopardize when you do not
 recognize "NOW".

The Spirit is the vehicle through which your thoughts
 transport energy of consciousness
to whatever your thoughts desire "NOW".

"NOW," think distinctively
of positive thoughts, loving, meaningful,
 peaceful, helpful, fruitful, healing, and joyful
 thoughts "NOW".

Then, you must command the Spirit to shine the light
 that guides the path
so you can achieve your purpose "NOW".

The SPIRIT will get you there
and it will make you shine at the perfect time "NOW".

Then, you must consciously be grateful for the
 mighty source,
that directs and guides the SPIRIT with such a powerful
 force through all the amazing thoughts "NOW."

ANOTHER SUNNY DAY

Yesterday was nice and sunny.
Paid all the bills, still had some money.
Felt so good I couldn't hide.
Went outside to clean my ride from top to bottom, and even inside.

With all the cleaning done,
time to go and have some fun.
With music playing loud and pumping,
suddenly I thought of something.
Not to spend this time alone,
I got my baby on the phone.
Ready for some fun today?
I'll pick you up along the way.
We were having so much fun couldn't dare miss out on none.
So, went downtown to have some rum.

Started acting like a creep,
out came some words I shouldn't speak.
So next to me became an empty seat.
People really start to peep.
As glass piled up in a heap, and because they seemed to
    know my name,
I'm really feeling shame, so out went my pride and fame.
Nothing said was really funny,
I just spent off all my money and left to part without my honey.

On that lonely ride back home, on my face I wore a frown,
the entire day turned upside down.
With so many worries in a heap, in my bed I lay and weep.
Didn't get much sleep, thoughts were wide and deep.

Have to work to pay the price,
so early morning had to rise.
Time to start another week.
Feeling draggy and fatigued, to the CREATOR I have to speak,
asking HIM to grant me peace,
and to fill my mind with ease.
So, have to tell HIM thanks and please,
cause with sunshine HE gave me these.

THAT'S A PLUS

Strongly living life trying to survive the hustle
    and bustle,
the ups and downs of everyday hassle.
Stop, take a deep breath, relax your muscle, life is not
    always a hassle.
That's a plus.
Must stop, take a few deep breaths.
Relax your brain, no need for all the unnecessary pain.
Free your mind, life is divine.
That's a plus.
Just think, just the other day you were very happy about
    what had happened.
Your face was lit up with a smile because you
    were so happy.
So, keep smiling, be happy.
That's a big plus.

AFTER ALL THESE YEARS

After all these years we live our lives waiting for the best years to come.
After all these years we love, we fuss, we get upset, we laugh, and we love again.
After all these years we work, we plan, we hurt no one, always aiming to be the best we can,
waiting for the best years to come.
After all these years our life is like an everlasting dream coming true,
waiting for the best years to come.
After all these years while we were dreaming, suddenly something has awakened us,
and the dream has now turned into reality.
Now we watch most of the world around us living in reality, showing no love, no care, going nowhere after all these years.
Let's take a break from all the stress.
More laugh, less cuss, and change the things we hate the most among us.
Let's stop the fuss and learn to share the things we love the most among us.
Then let's care, let's share, and fill the world with love and laughter.
Then, let's stop the time so there can be no after.
Then let's all go to sleep again so we can dream of peace and love again.
Waiting for the best years to come after all these years.

POWER FACTS

A horse only needs a shoe on a rocky road,
but not in a green pasture on solid ground.

Beauty is in the eye of the beholder, but remember to be humble and wise,
because the beheld's eye doesn't always see the same.

You can lead a horse to water but never you dare force it to drink.
Why do you think some see the truth while others do not?

A smile and a good gesture go a very long way,
so, smile and make it a special day today.

PROUD PARENTS

Parents, please listen to your children when they are crying out.
Show them love, be patient, take time and listen to what they are feeling.
Don't assume they don't know what they are saying.
If you listen to them, they, in return, will learn how to listen to you, also.
And, if you show them respect, they, in return, will show you respect, too.
Most children learn to identify themselves through their parents, so teach them well.
Do your best to set a great example.
Always share with them your loving heart.
They will share theirs with others, and you will always be a proud parent.

SHIFTED UNIVERSE

The universe has shifted.
This is the wide awakening.
We are in cleansing mode.
It's inevitable.
After the storm there will be a calm.
Know thyself in this time.
Stand firm.
Be caring to all living things.
We are entering an amazing time.
Be GRATEFULL!

IT'S A NEW DAY

Each morning when I rise, I look in the mirror, and I give thanks for what I see.
There was no charge from the CREATOR. HE created me all for free.
And when it was time for knowledge and wisdom, a whole heap was given to me.

So, to all the naysayers I'm proud to say, please move and get out the way.
My soul is hard-core, I'm definitely not here to play.
Like having a hot bowl of porridge, has given me courage, as challenging as it may.
There's a beacon of light that always shines bright, so I'm granted guidance along the way.

I unload all the baggage and refill them with knowledge, so it's not hard for me to say,
with a smile on my face, I can tell you the truth,
it's exciting to start another brand-new day.

CEASE AND SETTLE

Took a little cease from the writing and settle to practice
    and activate
these words of wisdom which I speak.
Must be conscious moving forward with every footstep
    that I take
as I place another feet.
Will be sharing conscious thoughts
with all the people I meet.
With this power that I am giving, truly special
and unique.
Be no resting on this journey till I reach the
maximum peak.
So joyful others are willing to listen truly inspires
me to teach.

www.ingramcontent.com/pod-product-compliance
Lightning Source LLC
Chambersburg PA
CBRC091123010526
44110CB00007B/181